Chad and Brad

Written by
Debbie Strayer

Illustrations by
Joy Majewski

New Sounds:

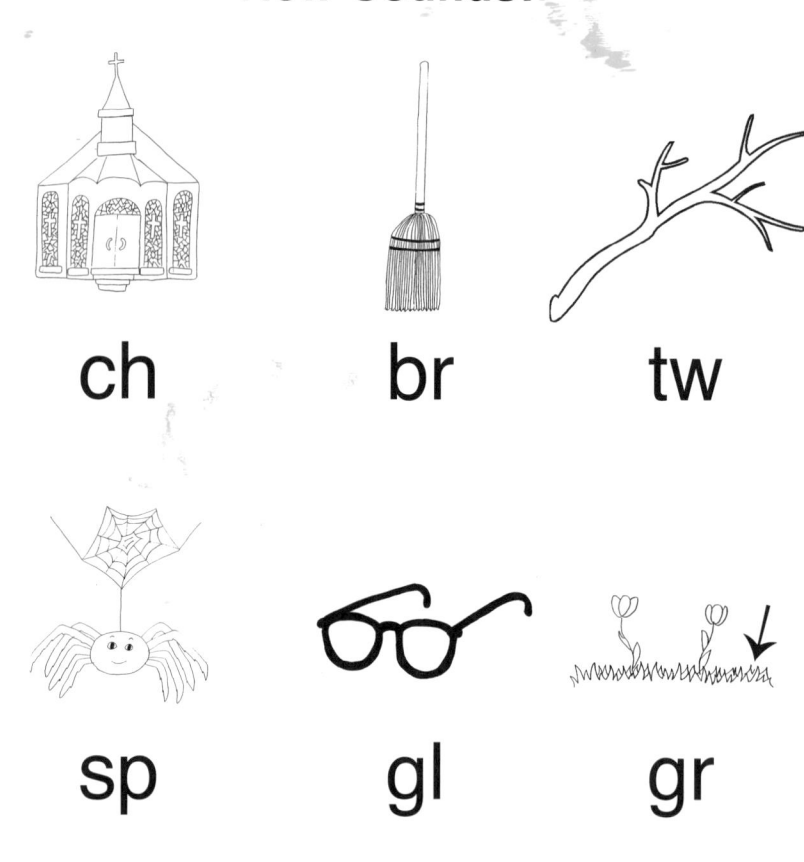

ch   br   tw

sp   gl   gr

(Note: The pictures indicate the sound, not the spelling.)

Common Sense Press

© 1998 by Common Sense Press

Printed 09/15

8786 Highway 21 • Melrose, FL 32666

ISBN 1-880892-59-6

Here are Chad and Brad. They are twins.

They like to chat with Tad. They sit on a branch.

The branch is brown.
It is not a twig!

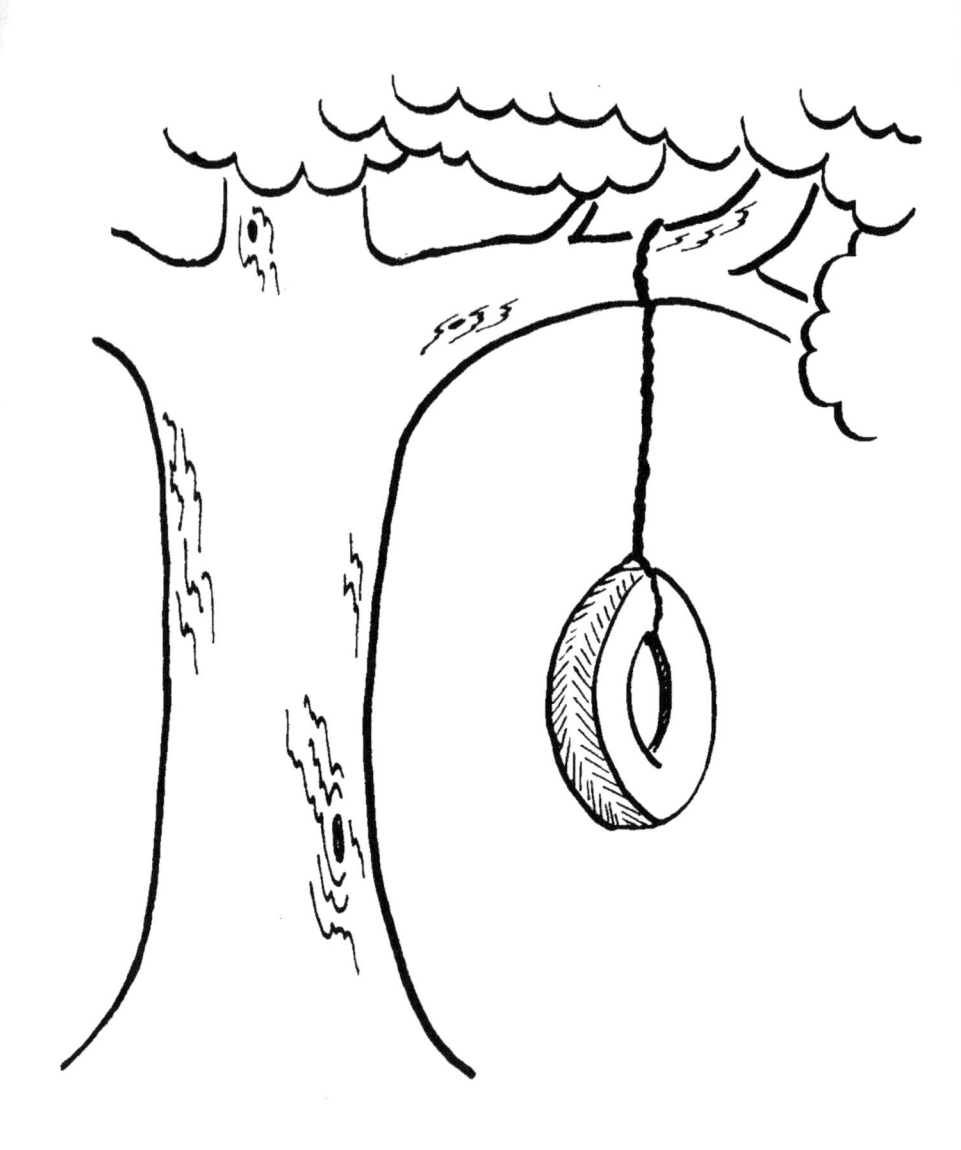

That rig can spin.
The lads are glad.

The big cat is Spat.
He will not spin.

Tad is sad. The rig hit his chin.

Brad sat on the rig.
See him grin.

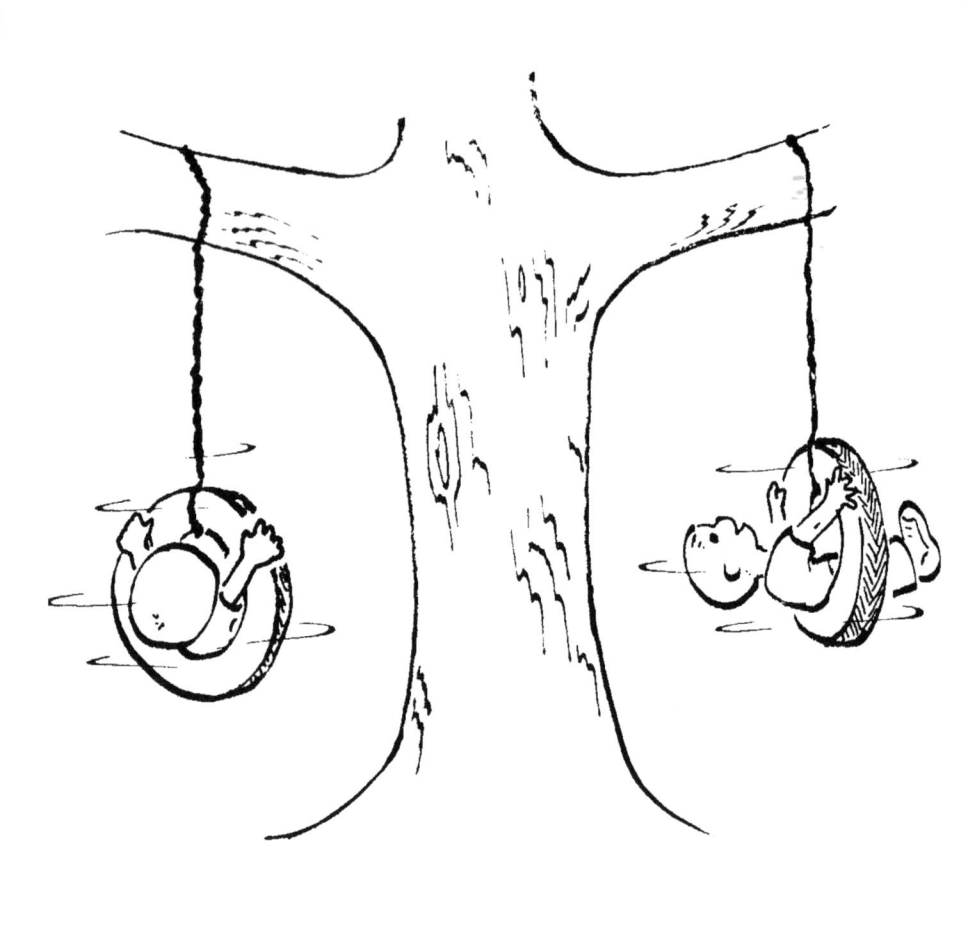

Chad likes to spin.
His rig will win.

New Words:

ch	br	tw	sp	gl	gr
Chad	Brad	twins	spin	glad	grin
chat		twig	spat		
chin					

Tad   sit   rig   lads

New Sight Words:

branch   brown   see   his
that   he   likes

9

Review Words:

to	will	not	can	sat
a	it	on	cat	sad
they	is	with	big	and
here	hit	the	win	are
him				